STUDY GUIDE

FINDING ANSWERS TO LIFE'S BIG QUESTIONS

Published by *iShine* Ministries, Sherman, TX, 75091 / ishinelive.com

ISBN: 978-0-9981658-0-6
Written by Robert Noland for 517 Resources, Inc. (in association with WTA Services)
Edited by Christy Distler
Design by Amy Balamut
Printed in the United States of America

TABLE OF CONTENTS

HOW TO USE THIS STUDY

The *Shock & Awe Study Guide,* based on *iShine's* live event, is an apologetics resource designed to engage students with the essential truths that are the foundation of our Christian beliefs. These four pillars from our faith can educate today's generation of young people to embrace a worldview based on the Bible. Here are a few tips to help this study be productive and efficient.

For Small Groups:

The format is designed to be as user-friendly as possible for parents, one-on-one mentors, and small and large group facilitators. Sections are clearly marked with exactly what to do: **SAY, READ,** and **DISCUSS.**

SAY sections—This material will work best and connect most with students if, in your preparation, you can familiarize yourself to the point of putting this content into your own words and making it your own. But you may also read these sections, if you choose.

READ sections—For accuracy of the information in these sections, we recommend you read these aloud as they are written. For the Bible verses, feel free to use your version of Scripture if you prefer. Just be certain the wording fits the topic context.

DISCUSS sections—You may use all the questions or only the ones you feel best fit your group. You can also customize questions of your own to fit your members' needs. The true goal of any small group or one-on-one meeting is to get everyone sharing, processing, and engaging with the topics.

There are two paths you may take in using this study:

1—The Comprehensive Path
For on-going settings such as small groups, Sunday school, or discipleship times where the material can be covered over multiple meetings, this format can be utilized by covering *all* the material in each session, ignoring the key icons. Be sure to factor in plenty of discussion time. For optimum ministry to be accomplished, we recommend reflection and ap-

plication times be offered to allow everyone to process and share what God is speaking to their hearts through the teaching.

2—The Key Points Path

This path offers an abbreviated version for time-sensitive situations where there is either shorter time frames or more students to discuss the material. We have marked the major points with a ⚿ icon and a corresponding line running down the side of the text to indicate where this key content starts and stops. If you are pressed for time at any point during the study, simply jump to the key points and follow the lines, skipping any content in between. This path ensures your students will get the big ideas of each session. If at all possible at another time, we encourage that the other content be covered to ensure they have received the full benefit of the *Shock & Awe Study*. This can be done in a future setting with you, or at home with their parents or alone.

For Self-Study:

While this study has been written with direction for small group or one-on-one facilitation, it also makes a great self-study resource for mature students. The facilitation language is simple and easily understandable when the study is approached individually. The space after each discussion question is provided for writing answers. A separate journal can also be used if more space is desired. Please read the small group tips above for best use of the various sections.

Settings to Use the Shock & Awe Study

Parent-Child	Small Group Meetings
Sunday School	Retreats
Discipleship Weekends	Youth Camps
Home School Meetings	Wednesday Night Youth Group
One-on-One Discipleship Courses	

INTRODUCTION

We began *iShine* after becoming convinced that no other age or stage of life is more crucial today than the tween years. Barna Group's research has confirmed that 90 percent of children form their lifelong beliefs before the end of their thirteenth year. This sobering stat means if a preteen has not made a faith commitment to Christ before the end of their eighth-grade year, the chances drop to just 1 in 10 that they will ever make such a decision.

We are all aware of the major shifts occurring in our society as the fault lines of seismic change are being exposed and shaking our very foundation, affecting the family and the church more than at any other time in modern history. We can no longer assume that our "church kids" are going to grasp their Christian heritage and carry it into adulthood. Any belief system is always just one generation away from extinction and, today, Christianity is no exception.

Now is the time to engage tweens and teens with intentional and respectful discussion, sincerely connecting with them regarding their beliefs to guide them in examining the essential pillars of our faith. We created this Shock & Awe Study to build a bridge between today's younger generation and their Christian foundation.

But without you, this is only a book of words. You, empowered by the Holy Spirit, will connect this study to the hearts of your group. The efforts of sincere and committed disciples, like you, can ensure that the biblical heritage of Christ's kingdom will be passed from this generation to the next.

Thank you for your investment in this generation through this resource. Thank you for spending your time and energy in ministry to students! May God richly bless and strengthen you in your service and labor of His love.

Pastor Brad Mathias   *iShine* Founder Robert Beeson

WHAT IF THERE IS A GOD?

INTRODUCTION:

Begin by accessing and watching the opening video. Below we have provided both a QR code (accessible by a phone or tablet via a QR reader app) and a web link to type into an Internet browser. Should you not have access to the web, the basic script is also below.

After you watch the first section of the video, instructions will appear on the screen that says "Pause Program Now." Pause the video, allowing the logo to stay on the screen during the session. When you have completed the session, click play on the video to watch the closing segment.

http://ishinelive.com/shockandawepart1/

Welcome to iShine's *Shock & Awe*. We're really excited you've decided to join us. The first thing we want you to know is that this study was created for you.

Questions. We've all got them—all the time. Questions like:

- How much data do I have left on my phone this month?
- Will my mom buy me those new shoes?
- Who can I hang with this weekend?

Then there are the tougher questions like:

- What if *my* parents get a divorce?
- What if we have to move before I graduate?
- Is my life going to just keep getting more stressful?

Then we zoom way out to the big picture. These are also the questions we can keep hidden deep inside of us that feel like secrets:

- Does my life really matter?
- What am I doing here anyway?
- Is this really all there is?

Being honest, we think about these questions a lot and stress over them more than we ever show. But wouldn't it be great to see if there are actually *real* answers? Like ones that might change your life?

What if you could settle some of the big life questions right now while you're young? What if life could make so much more sense down the road if you found some answers now?

So let's get started. The *Shock & Awe* Session 1 question is: What if there *is* a God?

STUDY START

 **SAY:**

Is there a God? A higher power? "Something" out there?

Or are we on our own? Is there actually nothing past this world with no real reason for our lives? Is there anything other than our mere existence for a few decades?

If there is no God, no Creator, no real purpose, then why shouldn't we all just look out for ourselves and squeeze everything we can from life, regardless of how it may affect others? Why should our behavior or decisions even matter, if this world is all there is?

Shock & Awe Study Guide

Scientists, historians, and even spiritual leaders throughout history all agree there are only two choices for how mankind got here:

1. Random chance—The world and all that we know *just happened*.
2. Intelligent design—There is a Creator with a master plan.

Believers in random chance offer no real answers for all the different species and elements, how complex our bodies are, and all that we see around us in the universe.

READ:

Sir Fred Hoyle, a British astronomer and author, made this statement about the creation of life being random: "The chance that higher life forms might have emerged in this way is comparable with the chance that a tornado sweeping through a junk yard might assemble a Boeing 747 from the materials therein."[1]

SAY:

While evolutionists and atheists debate and argue Hoyle's statement, he raises a strong analogy for the potential of our lives being random.

Even those who promote the Big Bang Theory—a sudden existence of the universe—have no explanation of what caused "the bang."

READ:

Sir Isaac Newton was a famous mathematician and scientist who believed strongly in God. The story is told that he had an atheist friend who, of course, did not believe in a Creator. One day, Sir Isaac went to a carpentry shop and asked the owner to make a model of our solar system. This model was to be to scale, intricately painted, and designed to resemble, as closely as possible, the actual solar system.

Several weeks later, Newton picked up the model, paid for it, and placed it in the center of a table in his house. Some time later, his atheist friend came over for a visit. When the friend arrived at Newton's house, the model of the solar system caught his eye, and he asked Sir Isaac if he could inspect it more closely. As the friend looked it over, he was awed by the fine craftsmanship and beauty. The atheist friend then asked Newton who had crafted this wonderful model of the solar system. Sir Isaac promptly replied that no one had made the model but that it had just appeared on his table one day, evidently by accident.

Confused, the friend asked the question again, and Newton repeated his answer that the model had come out of thin air. As the friend became frustrated, Sir Isaac then explained the purpose of his answer: If he could not convince his friend that this crude replica of the solar system had "just happened by accident," how could the friend believe that the real solar system, with all its complex design, could have appeared only by chance? The moral to the story: Design always demands a Designer. [2]

 ## SAY:

Every theory about man's origin has a beginning but no explanation as to what caused it—except one.

Of all the thousands of questions about our bodies that scientists have answered, there is a certain mystery that has never been successfully resolved: our fingerprints. Why do we have them? What's their biological purpose? Years of research have not produced a good answer.

While one study attempted to prove the purpose of fingerprints was to aid the grip of our fingers, another, a few years later, contradicted that study and concluded that the skin patterns actually reduce the contact area, making it harder to hold slick surfaces. Some scientists believe that fingerprints exist to improve our sense of touch. [3]

The only fact that *all* scientists agree on is that no two people's fingerprints are the same—even those of identical twins! Throughout all of human creation, no repetition of fingerprints has ever been found, with every set being original.

Well, if science cannot figure out what fingerprints are for or their origin, but no two are the same, then the next major question is *what* or *who* put them on us?

Here is yet another place in our creation equation where the subject of God, of a Creator, has to come up. Let's play "What if…?" for a second.

[The following are rhetorical questions, not meant for discussion.]

What if there is a God?

What if this God gave us our fingerprints?

Shock & Awe Study Guide

What if, like the painter's final brush strokes on the canvas, our Creator signs each of us with His customized signature?

What if God gave us fingerprints, making them unique to each one, simply to show us the great detail and care He takes in His creation?

DISCUSS:

- Why do you suppose people would want random chance to be the answer to creation? Why might that be a good choice to believe?

- What would be some differences in people who believe in intelligent design versus random chance?

- What did you think of Sir Fred Hoyle's tornado and 747 analogy? Discuss.

- What do *you* think our fingerprints say about us?

SAY:

Okay, that's the God factor, so let's go the other direction now. Random chance.

READ:

Evolution claims that non-living matter somehow became living organisms, which then changed over time and eventually gave birth to all living things we know today. This molecule-to-man theory states that hydrogen gas, if given enough time, will eventually turn into people.

Therefore, the evolutionist family tree looks like this in ascending order:
- Non-living matter
- Protozoa
- Metazoan invertebrates
- Vertebrate fishes
- Amphibians
- Reptiles
- Birds
- Fur-bearing quadrupeds
- Apes
- Man [4]

SAY:

Do you see how it takes just as much or even more faith to say reptiles made the successful leap to become birds and apes made the jump to become man, especially when there is no fossil evidence showing any forms that are in between two species?

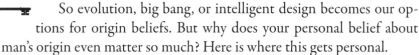 So evolution, big bang, or intelligent design becomes our options for origin beliefs. But why does your personal belief about man's origin even matter so much? Here is where this gets personal.

Who do you think might have the better self-image? Someone who believes that we are all a cosmic accident, morphed out of slime, and eventually evolved from apes? No point, no purpose, nothing personal? Random chance is the reason you exist?

But what about someone who believes a loving God intentionally planned and created him/her? An intentional creation with a purpose and even equipped with his/her own customized fingerprints!

What we believe about our own origin impacts everything we are—and aren't.

READ:

One of the greatest artists of all time was the sculptor and painter Michelangelo. In the early 1500s, when he was commissioned by the Catholic Church in Rome to paint the twelve apostles of Christ against a starry sky onto the ceiling of the Sistine Chapel, he asked if he could paint a more complex scheme. Over the next four years, Michelangelo painted nine episodes from Genesis onto the chapel ceiling, including over three hundred characters. He divided the artistic mural into four groups:
1. God's creation of the earth
2. God's creation of mankind
3. Man's fall from God's grace
4. God's redemption of man with the saving of Noah and his family. [5]

Today, you can still see Michelangelo's amazing work, which has been preserved over the centuries.

SAY:

Consider these three points regarding Michelangelo's artistic creation depicting God's work on behalf of mankind:

1. What if God has uniquely placed you into His painting of life to be a key character over the next several decades? He has artistically orchestrated your life, skills, gifts, talents, and qualities to be used in His masterpiece. You can choose to be all-in or all out. It's your call. He will not force you to believe in Him. But know this: God definitely believes in you and wants you in the picture, right there with Him, in the middle of His canvas.

2. What if God wants to use you to impact as much of the artistry of life and His vast canvas as you possibly can? He wants you to help Him bring others into His picture—to draw the lives of many into His kingdom through your life.

3. What if you are painted into His masterpiece, and yet He also allows you to be a painter with His hands guiding the brush. While God doesn't need you or me, He wants to insert and involve us in His story to change the world.

Let's look at Ephesians 2:10:

READ:

For we are God's masterpiece. He has created us anew in Christ Jesus, so we can do the good things he planned for us long ago. (NLT)

SAY:

See it? "He planned long ago." Like back at the beginning.
Let's take this verse apart and see what the Creator could be saying.
For we are God's masterpiece ...

If you have ever been to an art museum, then you know that the people who work there take special care to guard and protect all the works on display. Often the visitors are not even allowed to photograph the art because of the damage the flashes could impose. The reason they are so careful with these pieces is because of their extremely high value. Some works of art are worth millions, while some are considered invaluable, meaning that a dollar amount could never be placed on them. They are both invaluable *and* irreplaceable. The reason is because they are originals—one-of-a-kinds, deemed as masterpieces.

God created only *one* you. No one else has your exact walk, talk, smile, sense of humor, talents, thoughts, and ideas. You are God's masterpiece—invaluable *and* irreplaceable. No matter what you personally believe about yourself or what anyone else might tell you, God says those two adjectives are always *true* about you and describe *you*.

In this verse, the apostle Paul is clearly stating two things in these few words:

1.   You were God's concept all along. He thought you up. You were His idea. Certainly He used your parents to get you here, but *He* made you. Now you can certainly decide you won't believe that. You can buy into other ways and places where you came from, but the truth remains: God designed you.

2.   After He sketched you out with your specific design—which no one else has had, has, or ever will have, just like your fingerprints—He then formed you, created you. Check these verses out ...

⚷ READ:

Then God said, *"Let us make man in our image, in our likeness."* (Genesis 1:26)

For you created my inmost being; you knit me together in my mother's womb. I praise you because I am fearfully and wonderfully made; your works are wonderful, I know that full well. (Psalm 139:13–14)

SAY:

Let's go back to our fingerprints story. If someone does not believe in God or biblical creation, then fingerprints make no sense, because they cannot be explained. If one believes in God and that He created each person, unique fingerprints not only make perfect sense but also support the existence of the wonderful love and detailed care of a Creator.

⚷ Today, it is so easy to get lost in the masses of people and inside a mundane day-to-day experience, forgetting that you are completely unique, but there is just one you! Never forget this truth.

DISCUSS:

- Why does someone still have to show or express faith to believe in evolution?

- Who might have the better self-image—a random-chance or an intelligent-design believer? What are your thoughts?

- How do Ephesians 2:10, Genesis 1:26, and Psalm 139:13–14 support the idea of you being God's one-of-a-kind created work of art?

- Why would God's enemy, Satan, or the world *not* want you to see your true value?

- Why would God want you to see, as soon as possible in your life, that He created you for a purpose?

SAY:

Some of the biggest struggles in the tween, teen, and even college-age years are the search for two things:

1. Identity.

    Identity is who you truly are.

2. Approval.

    Approval is the permission to be who you are.

You need only one identity that encompasses all you are, and you need only one approval to be who you are.

The really good news for you today is that God offers you both identity *and* approval. God thought you up and then made you, so He sets you free to be exactly who He made you to be.

So you are God's concept, but He also wants you to be His companion, His friend. God walked with Adam and Eve in the Garden. The Bible says that Moses, Noah, David, and the great men and women of the faith walked with God. He wants you to walk with Him through life too.

Next, we're going to read Genesis 1:1–27. This is a long passage but crucial to our understanding of not only God's creation of the world but also His love and care for us. Remember, He didn't need this world; He created it for us.

READ:

In the beginning God created the heavens and the earth. The earth was formless and empty, and darkness covered the deep waters. And the Spirit of God was hovering over the surface of the waters.

Then God said, "Let there be light," and there was light. And God saw that the light was good. Then he separated the light from the darkness. God called the light "day" and the darkness "night."

And evening passed and morning came, marking the first day.

Then God said, "Let there be a space between the waters, to separate the waters of the heavens from the waters of the earth." And that is what happened. God made this space to separate the waters of the earth from the waters of the heavens. God called the space "sky."

And evening passed and morning came, marking the second day. Then God said, "Let the waters beneath the sky flow together into one place, so dry ground may appear." And that is what happened. God called the dry ground "land" and the waters "seas." And God saw that it was good. Then God said, "Let the land sprout with vegetation—every sort of seed-bearing plant, and trees that grow seed-bearing fruit. These seeds will then produce the kinds of plants and trees from which they came." And that is what happened. The land produced vegetation—all sorts of seed-bearing plants, and trees with seed-bearing fruit. Their seeds produced plants and trees of the same kind. And God saw that it was good.

And evening passed and morning came, marking the third day.

Then God said, "Let lights appear in the sky to separate the day from the night. Let them be signs to mark the seasons, days, and years. Let these lights in the sky shine down on the earth." And that is what happened. God made two great lights—the larger one to govern the day, and the smaller one to govern the night. He also made the stars. God set these lights in the sky to light the earth, to govern the day and night, and to separate the light from the darkness. And God saw that it was good.

And evening passed and morning came, marking the fourth day.

Then God said, "Let the waters swarm with fish and other life. Let the skies be filled with birds of every kind." So God created great sea creatures and every living thing that scurries and swarms in the water, and every sort of bird—each producing offspring of the same kind. And God saw that it was *good. Then God blessed them, saying, "Be fruitful and multiply. Let the fish fill the seas, and let the birds multiply on the earth."*

And evening passed and morning came, marking the fifth day.

Then God said, "Let the earth produce every sort of animal, each producing offspring of the same kind—livestock, small animals that scurry along the ground, and wild animals." And that is what happened. God made all sorts of wild animals, livestock, and small animals, each able to produce offspring of the same kind. And God saw that it was good.

Then God said, "Let us make human beings in our image, to be like us. They will reign over the fish in the sea, the birds in the sky, the livestock, all the wild animals on the earth, and the small animals that scurry along the ground."

So God created human beings in his own image. In the image of God he created them; male and female he created them. (NLT)

SAY:

Throughout your life people will try to teach you and convince you of various beliefs about the existence of man. Many people who go to church and claim to be Christians believe other theories rather than biblical creation. Some people will make statements such as, "I'm not sure I believe in God creating the world the way it says in Genesis, but I believe He had something to do with it. Even if it was slime that crawled up onto the land and evolved over time, He did it." Many want to believe God created the world, but they don't want to "limit themselves" to the way Scripture says it happened. This way, if any part of the Bible speaks against their lifestyle, they won't have to obey its words.

Let's look at more reasons why it is so important to you and your personal self-concept to believe the biblical account of creation.

Evolution and non-God origin theories remove the concept of personal responsibility for behavior. In other words, if you believe you are an accident, this strongly affects how you think about yourself and your future. If there is no point to life, why care about others and show love and kindness? Why not do what you want and have all the fun you can while you can? If you are your own standard, why should personal responsibility matter at all?

But how does a belief that a loving God created you and wants a relationship with you affect how you think about yourself and your future? A purpose for life means decisions and behavior will not only impact you but also those all around you.

The great news of the gospel is that God has always been involved in your life and always will be.

READ:

Then the Lord God formed a man from the dust of the ground and breathed into his nostrils the breath of life, and the man became a living being. (Genesis 2:7)

SAY:

Where was God in this scene? He was in the dirt—involved, creating, engaged. He breathed His own breath into Adam's nostrils. No one did "the dirty work" for God; He did it Himself!

God was giving, not taking. He has been giving life from the start and has never stopped.

And who took on the creation of Eve (woman) from Adam (man)? Once again, God Himself.

Let's make one truth clear ...

You were formed out of a deep love from a God who desperately loves you. You didn't come from apes. Your ancestors didn't crawl up onto the seashore out of primordial ooze. You didn't evolve or morph, and you certainly were not an accident. God planned, designed, and made you.

We read from Psalm 139 earlier, but let's repeat verses 13 and 14, while adding 15 and 16.

READ:

For you created my inmost being; you knit me together in my mother's womb. I praise you because I am fearfully and wonderfully made; your works are wonderful, I know that full well. My frame was not hidden from you when I was made in the secret place; when I was woven together in the depths of the

earth. Your eyes saw my unformed body; all the days ordained for me were written in your book before one of them came to be. (Psalm 139:13–16)

DISCUSS:

- Why is your identity—understanding who you are—so crucial to how you live your life?

- Why is approval from the right source so important? Or is it?

- If God did create you, why do you suppose He would want you to desire a relationship with Him?

- How might knowing that God was intimately involved in your creation, as we read in Genesis 2 and Psalm 139, help you find purpose for your life?

WRAP-UP:

When you have completed the session, hit play on the video link, taking the video off pause, to watch the closing segment. If you cannot access the video, the basic script is available below to close the session.

So God's Word is clear that He is all-in for you. He says He created you out of love and care for a purpose. And just like your fingerprints prove, there is only one you. No one is quite like you, so no one can fulfill your life's mission like you can—and will.

But what do you think? What do you believe? No one can make this choice for you. This is *your* decision.

The point of your own origin is one of the most significant decisions you will make, because this determines where you go for the answers that will define you for a lifetime.

What you believe about yourself also determines your actions. Your self-concept and your God-concept are crucial to how you will live.

The story is told of a young man who was desperate to find answers for his life, so he sought out the wisdom of an old pastor who lived in his neighborhood. As the talk turned toward God, the younger man said, "But I just can't seem to understand how to see God in this world." The older man responded quietly yet confidently, "Well, I have a very different perspective, for when I look at the same world, I cannot *not* see Him."

Everyone from the atheist to the Bible scholar has to agree on one major point in this discussion: The universe had to come to exist somehow. So each one of us must answer this question: What *if* there is a God?

WHAT IF THE BIBLE IS TRUE?

INTRODUCTION:

Begin by accessing and watching the opening video. Below we have provided both a QR code (accessible by a phone or tablet via a QR reader app) and a web link to type into an Internet browser. Should you not have access to the web, the basic script is also below.

After you watch the first section of the video, instructions will appear on the screen that says "Pause Program Now." Pause the video, allowing the logo to stay on the screen during the session. When you have completed the session, click play on the video to watch the closing segment.

http://ishinelive.com/shockandawepart2/

Welcome to iShine's *Shock & Awe,* the second session.

When someone says the word *Bible*, what do you think of? What images or ideas pop into your head? *Everyone* seems to have an opinion about this book. From conviction to controversy, fairy tales to facts, history book to heaven-sent. But why? Why does one single book create such a stir among humanity over thousands of years?

Well, a huge reason is because what other book claims to be the words of God Himself? What other book tells you who God is and how to get to heaven? And what other book offers you wisdom and advice on how He would have you live?

But none of this matters if the words on the pages are not true—if it's all just a big lie, a collection of myths and fables.

Maybe it's time for you to gather some evidence for yourself and decide what you believe. After all, what does it matter to you what anyone else says about the Bible? You're at a place in life where it's time for you to make some decisions that will affect your future. And the Bible ... well, this is an important one. What if the Bible is true? True ... to you ... for you?

STUDY START

 **SAY:**

For centuries, people have declared the Bible to be only a book of:
- History
- Myths
- Traditional teachings
- Spiritual fables
- Archaic and outdated laws and commands for the religious

In every generation, there are those who simply care nothing about the Bible and would never even consider reading its pages, much less applying the words to their lives. Then there are those who make it their mission to boldly and loudly declare the Bible to be a book of lies and deception.

Let's go with the idea that the Bible is just a man-made book, written by religious and well-meaning men to be an ancient text in which the generations can believe and use to provide hope. This idea means the Bible is *not* the Word of God and has no real link to any deity, eternity, or heaven. How might such a book help us? Is it a record of early history or just instructions and guidelines to live a more meaningful life?

Do these purposes for the Bible alone warrant it to be the best-selling book of all time? After all, many people do believe it is not *the* Word of God but still respect the words as some kind of sacred text with value for their lives.

But as you read Scripture, you come upon passages such as:

READ:

Love the Lord your God with all your heart and with all your soul and with all your strength. These commandments that I give you today are to be on your hearts. Impress them on your children. Talk about them when you sit at home and when you walk along the road, when you lie down and when you get up. Tie them as symbols on your hands and bind them on your foreheads. Write them on the doorframes of your houses and on your gates. (Deuteronomy 6:5–9)

Blessed is the one who does not walk in step with the wicked or stand in the way that sinners take or sit in the company of mockers, but whose delight is in the law of the Lord, and who meditates on his law day and night. That person is like a tree planted by streams of water, which yields its fruit in season and whose leaf does not wither—whatever they do prospers. (Psalm 1:1–3)

All Scripture is inspired by God and is useful to teach us what is true and to make us realize what is wrong in our lives. It corrects us when we are wrong and teaches us to do what is right. God uses it to prepare and equip his people to do every good work. (2 Timothy 3:16–17 NLT)

Because of that experience, we have even greater confidence in the message proclaimed by the prophets. You must pay close attention to what they wrote, for their words are like a lamp shining in a dark place—until the Day dawns, and Christ the Morning Star shines in your hearts. Above all, you must realize that no prophecy in Scripture ever came from the prophet's own understanding, or from human initiative. No, those prophets were moved by the Holy Spirit, and they spoke from God. (2 Peter 1:19–21 NLT)

SAY:

These passages appear to be God speaking *to us,* trying to communicate His love and care *for us.* But if the Bible is only a book written by men for us to live a better *life,* then what about *death?* There are hundreds of references to death and eternal life that we cannot ignore. Scripture appears to tell us how death creates a doorway to eternity, which is exactly what these words say God created us for.

DISCUSS:

- Why do you think some people claim the Bible is only a book of fables and myths?

- If someone doesn't believe the Bible is true, why might they want to devote their time and energy to refute it?

- In Deuteronomy 6:5–9, why do you think the writer would be so detailed as to how to keep God's Word the first priority?

- In Psalm 1:1–3, why might the writer contrast the "wicked, sinners, and mockers" to the person who follows God's Word? What promise does he make?

- In 2 Timothy 3:16–17, what claims are made about the Bible's connection to God?

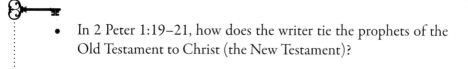

- In 2 Peter 1:19–21, how does the writer tie the prophets of the Old Testament to Christ (the New Testament)?

READ:

Over the centuries, many people have questioned the Bible's accuracy. Here are four facts to consider:

- Forty authors over 1,400 years are responsible for the final sixty-six books of the Bible. Scribes originally penned the words onto large parchments contained on heavy scrolls.
- To maintain accuracy in the copies that were created, when a page was completed, the copy was placed onto an original and if the center word on the page did not match up exactly, the copy page was burned and the scribe would start over.
- Only four hundred words are in question in the New Testament regarding their original composition, creating a 99.9 percent accuracy rate. None of those four hundred words are related to actual doctrine.
- Twenty-four thousand known copies of the original New Testament are still in existence today, with the oldest copy being only one hundred years from the original. Many other known ancient texts span up to five hundred years from the original to the oldest copy, allowing for more potential deviation. [6]

Wycliffe Bible Translators provide the following facts about current availability of Scripture:

- Approximately 550 languages have the complete translated Bible.
- Approximately 1,300 languages have access to the New Testament and some portions of Scripture in their language.
- Approximately 2,300 languages across 130 countries have active translation and linguistic development work being done today. [7]

SAY:

If the Bible is just a humanly inspired, man-driven book, why, in its formative years, was it so meticulously handled with such careful oversight and artistry? Even today, what other book receives so much global attention and is continually under constant translation in multiple languages with people dedicating years of their lives to its conversion?

Let's flip to the other side and look at the Bible as actually being God's Word—provided *to* man, *through* man, *for* man.

The Bible continually claims to be God's:

• **Prophecy**

READ:

The Encyclopedia of Bible Prophecy states there are 1,239 prophecies in the Old Testament and 578 in the New Testament, encompassing 8,352 verses. [8] While we find theologians differing on the actual number of prophecies that Christ fulfilled, all agree there are direct and exact connections to many of these.

Here are two great examples—one for Jesus' birth and one for His death.

All right then, the Lord himself will give you the sign. Look! The virgin will conceive a child! She will give birth to a son and will call him Immanuel (which means 'God is with us'). (Isaiah 7:14 NLT)

SAY:

Most theologians believe this prophecy was made about seven hundred years before Christ's birth. Verses such as this were exactly why people were watching and waiting for the Messiah, because while many details of His coming were specific, God didn't say *when* He would come!

And His death ...

READ:

My life is poured out like water, and all my bones are out of joint. My heart is like wax, melting within me. My strength has dried up like sunbaked clay. My tongue sticks to the roof of my mouth. You have laid me in the dust and left me for dead. My enemies surround me like a pack of dogs; an evil gang closes in on me. They have pierced my hands and feet. I can count all my bones. My enemies stare at me and gloat. They divide my garments among themselves and throw dice for my clothing. (Psalm 22:14–18 NLT)

SAY:

This was written approximately one thousand years prior to Christ's death, before the brutal practice of crucifixion was even used! The language obviously describes Christ's thirst-parched, nail-pierced body, even down to the centurions gambling for his robe at the foot of the cross, as described in Luke 23.

If the Bible is God's Word, then He used these many connections throughout history to prove to us that He is real and His Son is who He said He is.

- **Precepts**

If God created us, then He would also know the best way to live life. His Word would be filled with instructions to protect us. The most well known are the Ten Commandments found in Exodus 20 and Deuteronomy 5.

Jesus was once asked a very interesting question, by a religious official, about God's precepts, found in Matthew 22:35–39.

READ:

One of them, an expert in the law, tested him with this question: "Teacher, which is the greatest commandment in the Law?" Jesus replied: "'Love the Lord your God with all your heart and with all your soul and with all your mind.' This is the first and greatest commandment. And the second is like it: 'Love your neighbor as yourself.'"

SAY:

Knowing the Pharisees were trying to trap him by His own words, Jesus simply summed up all of God's laws into this (paraphrasing): "Love God, love others, and love yourself—in that order."

- **Principles**

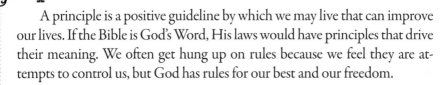

A principle is a positive guideline by which we may live that can improve our lives. If the Bible is God's Word, His laws would have principles that drive their meaning. We often get hung up on rules because we feel they are attempts to control us, but God has rules for our best and our freedom.

Let's look at two of God's ten laws—one about Him and one about us—to find the real principle offering His meaning for our lives.

Exodus 20:3 states, *"You shall have no other gods before me."* Many read this verse and believe God to be power-hungry and self-centered. That mindset places on Him human sinful qualities, which He does not have.

So we must ask why a loving Creator would tell us to not place anyone before Him. While there are many reasons given and passages provided, read Proverbs 4:10–13:

READ:

My child, listen to me and do as I say, and you will have a long, good life. I will teach you wisdom's ways and lead you in straight paths. When you walk, you won't be held back; when you run, you won't stumble. Take hold of my instructions; don't let them go. Guard them, for they are the key to life. (NLT)

God knows anyone or anything else we try to follow will lead us down the wrong path. We were created by Him, and for Him; therefore *He* is our only God.

Let's look at Exodus 20:13: *"You shall not murder."*

Why would the Creator of life tell us not to murder each other? Because the act of murder is to hate someone to the point of wanting them dead. Murder is permanently taking over the authority of someone's life, which we were never meant to have. To kill a person is not to love life, and God created us to love each other and be a source of life, not death. This principle of always choosing life over death is the driving force for the sixth commandment.

As He so often did, Jesus took the Old Testament teachings to a deeper place. In Matthew 5:21–22, He warns against starting down the road to murder by avoiding the first step—unrighteous anger.

READ:

"You have heard that our ancestors were told, 'You must not murder. If you commit murder, you are subject to judgment.' But I say, if you are even angry with someone, you are subject to judgment!"

SAY:

A perfect God has perfect principles—solid and wise reasons—behind every precept.

- **Promises**

From prophecy to precepts to principles, we get to the one we tend to like the most—God's promises to us. While there are literally hundreds found throughout Scripture, here are a few often-quoted and familiar ones.

READ:

But those who trust in the Lord will find new strength. They will soar high on wings like eagles. They will run and not grow weary. They will walk and not faint. (Isaiah 40:31 NLT)

"For I hold you by your right hand—I, the Lord your God. And I say to you, 'Don't be afraid. I am here to help you.'" (Isaiah 41:13 NLT)

"For I know the plans I have for you," declares the Lord, "plans to prosper you and not to harm you, plans to give you hope and a future." (Jeremiah 29:11)

"And be sure of this: I am with you always, even to the end of the age." (Matthew 28:20 NLT)

SAY:

God desires a relationship with us and tells us clearly throughout Scripture the benefits of following Him in obedience.

DISCUSS:

- Why do you think so many people view God's precepts, laws, and commandments as bad or bothersome?

- Why would a *loving* God want to give His creation precepts or rules to follow? Why would a *just* God want to do this?

- Why might God want us to understand the principles—the whys—behind His precepts and laws?

- Why do we tend to read and quote God's promises more than His prophecies, precepts, and principles?

READ:

There was a day when the idea of every family, let alone every Christian, owning their own Bible would have been unthinkable. In the mid-1400s, Johann Gutenberg developed the first method of mass-produced printing. He printed the Bible on six presses with forty-two lines per page. Approximately two hundred copies were completed with the letters resembling the style of the scribes who had always created copies in the past. By the late 1400s, every European country had at least one printing press. [9] This soon allowed the Bible to be the most printed book in history, with copies made available for the first time to people other than just scholars and monks. Slowly, the Bible became available to all English-speaking people.

Fast-forward to today when Bibles sit on shelves in countless Western-culture homes, especially in the United States. Today, if you stacked all the Bibles in American homes on top of each other, they would rise to 29 million feet—nearly one thousand times the height of Mount Everest. According to the Barna Group, more than 90 percent of American households own a Bible and the average family owns three. Today, 1.5 billion Gideon Bibles are in hotel rooms. Year after year, the Bible outsells any other book, regardless of the state of the economy. [10]

SAY:

But we all know that simply owning a book or having it sit in our home doesn't change anything.

What might happen if everyone in America agreed to live by the principles of the Bible, even if they didn't believe in God, Jesus, or heaven? Could things be changed in our nation, simply by people applying the truth of Scripture?

But if God's Word is accurate and trustworthy—if it is truly God's Word to mankind, alive and used by His Spirit in our lives—this could revolutionize anyone who reads and applies its truth.

Even if everyone in the nation, your city, community, and neighborhood adjusted their lives to the Bible, this still will not change you. The only way you will change is if you decide for yourself that God's Word is the foundation for *your own* life and future. Then you can impact anyone and everyone by the life you lead.

WRAP-UP:

When you have completed the session, hit play on the video link, taking the video off pause, to watch the closing segment. If you cannot access the video, the basic script is available below to close the session.

If the Bible tells the story of God and mankind, then your story must be in its pages as well. No, not your actual name, but whenever the words *we, our,* and *your,* as well as terms like *children of God,* are used, they are about you—they include you.

Every day in every American home, so much of what is delivered to our mailboxes is junk mail—advertisements and offers, mostly wanting our money. The words of these letters and ads are not personal; the words are not written to us but to whoever opens the envelope. So we toss them out because they aren't special or meaningful. This is how a lot of people see the Bible—kind of like junk mail.

But then what if you get an envelope in the mail, addressed by hand just to you. You open it, and someone has handwritten you a letter. The words are very personal and intimate. They're only about you, telling you what you mean to the writer and how much that person loves you. That's exactly why we call those "love letters." You keep those, and you read and re-read them.

If the Bible is from God, about your life, then that's how you can see the Bible—God's love letter to you, about you, and for you. But love letters are only love letters if you truly believe the words written by the sender. And they're the most special when you love the person who wrote you. So what do you believe about the Bible? Just stories or *your* story? Junk mail or love letter? You decide.

WHAT IF JESUS IS WHO HE CLAIMED TO BE?

INTRODUCTION:

Begin by accessing and watching the opening video. Below we have provided both a QR code (accessible by a phone or tablet via a QR reader app) and a web link to type into an Internet browser. Should you not have access to the web, the basic script is also below.

After you watch the first section of the video, instructions will appear on the screen that says "Pause Program Now." Pause the video, allowing the logo to stay on the screen during the session. When you have completed the session, click play on the video to watch the closing segment.

http://ishinelive.com/shockandawepart3/

Welcome to iShine *Shock & Awe's* third session.

Well, if the Bible is considered controversial, that's nothing compared to the debates and discussions about Jesus Christ. But just like in His day, it seems to be the religious and the scholars who argue and debate Him, while the common folks like you and me are just amazed at what He taught and what He did in His three-year ministry.

But yet, being amazed at miracles and teaching doesn't change our lives, does it? We can watch an awesome movie with incredible effects and storyline, but that doesn't mean we think it's real or that we have found something on which to base our lives.

Jesus made a lot of claims about the future, as well as connections to the past. He said He was the fulfillment of the Old Testament prophecies and also would be forever seated at the right hand of God in heaven.

All these add up to Jesus being who He claimed to be ... or ... the biggest liar in history. No one has ever made the statements that He did, but no one has ever been witnessed to rise from the dead and ascend to heaven either!

So if there is a God—if the Bible is true—then could this God-man truly be the Savior of the world? And could He be *your* Savior? *Your* Lord?

Let's get started. What if Jesus is who He claimed to be? What do you say?

STUDY START

 **SAY:**

The best way to begin in any discussion about Jesus Christ is to first make one key point clear: the majority of historians, regardless of their spiritual leanings, agree He was a real person who actually existed. Most respected and reputable experts throughout the centuries believed Jesus was quite real, not just a myth or legend. His birth, life, and death are a matter of public record. The academic and historical world attests to this fact.

READ:

Cornelius Tacitus lived from 56 to 120 AD and is among the most trusted of ancient historians. Serving under Roman Emperor Vespasian as a senator, he was also proconsul of Asia. In what is known as the Annals of 116 AD, he details Emperor Nero's claim that the Christians were to blame for the great fire in Rome. Tacitus wrote: "Consequently, to get rid of the report, Nero fastened the guilt and inflicted the most exquisite tortures on a class hated for their abominations, called Christians by the populace. Christus, from whom the name had its origin, suffered the extreme penalty during the reign of Tiberius at the hands of one of our procurators, Pontius Pilatus, and a most mischievous superstition, thus checked for the moment, again broke out not only in Judea, the first source of the evil, but even in Rome, where all things hideous and shameful from every part of the world find their centre and become popular." [11]

SAY:

Note that Tacitus's language was sarcastic and hostile toward Christ and His followers. He had no agenda to prove Christianity in reporting these facts, and his personal opinion clearly comes through.

Three references are found here:
- Christ's followers were first known as Christians.
- Christ's capital punishment was "the extreme penalty" of the day, referring to crucifixion.
- Pontius Pilate was the official to sentence Jesus.

READ:

One of the most read and quoted historians to provide details about Christ was Josephus, who lived from 37–101 AD. He was actually writing a history of the Jews but included passages about Christianity. He wrote, "Now around this time lived Jesus, a wise man. For he was a worker of amazing deeds and was a teacher of people who gladly accept the truth. He won over both many Jews and many Greeks. Pilate, when he heard him accused by the leading men among us, condemned him to the cross, (but) those who had first loved him did not cease (doing so). To this day the tribe of Christians named after him has not disappeared." [12]

SAY:

Josephus's language is much more positive toward Christ and the new movement that was obviously growing. However, again, this is simply a historian's report.

Three references are found here:

- Christ performed miracles.
- Pilate sentenced Jesus.
- Christianity grew following the resurrection.

While there are many other historians' quotes available to us regarding Christ, this sampling shows us that Jesus' existence is proven *outside* the Bible.

But what about Jesus claiming to be God? First, we must look at what kinds of claims He actually made.

READ:

The woman said, "I know that Messiah" (called Christ) "is coming. When he comes, he will explain everything to us." Then Jesus declared, "I, the one speaking to you—I am he." (John 4:25–26)

Jesus said to them, "If God were your Father, you would love me, for I have come here from God. I have not come on my own; God sent me." (John 8:42)

Thomas said to him, "Lord, we don't know where you are going, so how can we know the way?" Jesus answered, "I am the way and the truth and the life. No one comes to the Father except through me. If you really know me, you will know my Father as well. From now on, you do know him and have seen him." (John 14:5–7)

SAY:

We can see in many Scripture passages, as we just read, that Jesus made clear and direct statements about being sent by and from God.

What kinds of things did He do to prove He was not an ordinary human but the Son of God?

READ:

The royal official said, "Sir, come down before my child dies." "Go," Jesus replied, "your son will live." The man took Jesus at his word and departed. While he was still on the way, his servants met him with the news that his boy was living. When he inquired as to the time when his son got better, they said to him, "Yesterday, at one in the afternoon, the fever left him." Then the father realized that this was the exact time at which Jesus had said to him, "Your son will live." So he and his whole household believed. (John 4:49–53)

Another of his disciples, Andrew, Simon Peter's brother, spoke up, "Here is a boy with five small barley loaves and two small fish, but how far will they go among so many?" Jesus said, "Have the people sit down." There was plenty of grass in that place, and they sat down (about five thousand men were there). Jesus then took the loaves, gave thanks, and distributed to those who were seated as much as they wanted. He did the same with the fish. When they had all had enough to eat, he said to his disciples, "Gather the pieces that are left over. Let nothing be wasted." So they gathered them and filled twelve baskets with the pieces of the five barley loaves left over by those who had eaten. (John 6:8–13)

When evening came, his disciples went down to the lake, where they got into a boat and set off across the lake for Capernaum. By now it was dark, and Jesus had not yet joined them. A strong wind was blowing and the waters grew rough. When they had rowed about three or four miles, they saw Jesus approaching the boat, walking on the water; and they were frightened. But he said to them, "It is I; don't be afraid." (John 6:16–20)

SAY:

We would all likely agree that resurrecting a dying child, multiplying a lunch into a huge banquet, and walking on water in a storm are equal to God-sized events. All these occurred before many witnesses, especially the feeding of more than five thousand people.

How did people respond to Jesus' ministry and claims?

⚷— READ:

Then, leaving her water jar, the woman went back to the town and said to the people, "Come, see a man who told me everything I ever did. Could this be the Messiah?" ... Many of the Samaritans from that town believed in him because of the woman's testimony, "He told me everything I ever did." (John 4:28–29, 39)

Now there was a Pharisee, a man named Nicodemus who was a member of the Jewish ruling council. He came to Jesus at night and said, "Rabbi, we know that you are a teacher who has come from God. For no one could perform the signs you are doing if God were not with him." (John 3:1–2)

So, because Jesus was doing these things on the Sabbath, the Jewish leaders began to persecute him. ... For this reason they tried all the more to kill him. (John 5:16–18)

SAY:

Many believed, some were just curious with their questions, and others became hostile and wanted to stop Him. This is still true to this day. The only other response we might add in today's culture is apathy, or simply not caring.

DISCUSS:

- After reading historians' claims of Jesus performing miracles and "amazing deeds," do you think it is possible He was merely a magician or a holy man, yet not actually God? Why or why not?

- Why would Jesus' many claims to be the Messiah mean He is either truly God or a crazed liar? Why do His statements not leave room for an in-between possibility?

- How might some people explain Jesus' miracles outside of Him being God?

- Why do you think people would believe in Jesus' miracles and follow His teaching, yet not actually trust that He has the power to save souls?

- Why do you think people can look at the same evidence about Jesus, yet come up with very different responses or conclusions? What causes this?

SAY:

Next, let's look at the birth and resurrection of Christ. If Jesus is who He claimed to be, then these were the greatest historical and spiritual events in the history of mankind. Regardless of anyone's opinions, Christmas is still the most celebrated holiday in the world, and *all of history* is separated and dated by His birth and death—BC (before Christ) and AD (anno Domini/in the year of the Lord).

As we already discussed in the second session on the Bible, prophecies were recorded in Scripture that speak of Christ's birth, death, and resurrection. Isaiah prophesied His birth around seven hundred years before the event occurred.

READ:

For to us a child is born, to us a son is given, and the government will be on his shoulders. And he will be called Wonderful Counselor, Mighty God, Everlasting Father, Prince of Peace. (Isaiah 9:6)

SAY:

Regarding the resurrection, the first Old Testament prophecy referred to in this passage is found in Psalm 16:8–10, and, like the Isaiah passage, was written long before Christ's birth.

READ:

I have placed the Lord always in front of me. Because He is at my right hand, I will not be moved. And so my heart is glad. My soul is full of joy. My body also will rest without fear. For You will not give me over to the grave. And You will not allow Your Holy One to return to dust. (NLV)

SAY:

Jesus' body didn't stay in the grave, and His body experienced no decay. In fact, quite the opposite happened; He was brought back to life in a heavenly body. Christ's mission in coming to earth—from birth to death to resurrection—was foretold by God's prophets and recorded in the Old Testament hundreds of years earlier. The story of Christ is interwoven throughout the *entire* Bible.

There are striking similarities between Christ's birth and His resurrection. Angels were present and very involved in *both* events.

First, at His birth ...

READ:

And there were shepherds living out in the fields nearby, keeping watch over their flocks at night. An angel of the Lord appeared to them, and the glory of the Lord shone around them. ... Suddenly a great company of the heavenly host appeared with the angel, praising God and saying, "Glory to God in the highest heaven, and on earth peace to those on whom his favor rests." (Luke 2:8–9, 13–14)

The messenger angel:
1) Told the shepherds to not be afraid
2) Made God's announcement

3) Invited them to go and see Jesus after telling them where to find Him

Now to the resurrection …

After the Sabbath, at dawn on the first day of the week, Mary Magdalene and the other Mary went to look at the tomb. There was a violent earthquake, for an angel of the Lord came down from heaven and, going to the tomb, rolled back the stone and sat on it. His appearance was like lightning, and his clothes were white as snow. The guards were so afraid of him that they shook and became like dead men. The angel said to the women, "Do not be afraid, for I know that you are looking for Jesus, who was crucified." (Matthew 28:1–5)

Here we see an angel making another announcement of good news regarding Jesus. Look at the pattern here.

The messenger angel:

1) Told the women to not be afraid
2) Made God's announcement
3) Invited them to go and see Jesus after telling them where to find Him

SAY:

Amazing, right? The angels' identical appearances give us yet another assurance that Jesus' coming was God's doing. This was the fulfillment of His plan.

Now, check this out. Do you remember what Jesus was wrapped in as a baby after His birth?

READ:

She wrapped him in cloths and placed him in a manger, because there was no guest room available for them. (Luke 2:7)

Now, look at the resurrection …

So Peter and the other disciple started for the tomb. Both were running, but the other disciple outran Peter and reached the tomb first. He bent over and looked in at the strips of linen lying there but did not go in. Then Simon Peter came along behind him and went straight into the tomb. He saw the <u>strips of linen lying there, as well as the cloth that had been wrapped around</u>

Jesus' head. The cloth was still lying in its place, separate from the linen. (*John 20:3–7, underline added*)

Let's take an A-B look to compare some other key factors that match Jesus' birth to His resurrection:

Birth—The shepherds were very important in the story of Christ's birth because they were the first eyewitnesses, both of the angels and of Jesus.

Resurrection—The disciples were crucial in Christ's resurrection because they were among the first witnesses. Many had seen His horrible death just three days before.

Birth—The shepherds were excited and full of emotion as they ran to see Jesus and tell others.

Resurrection—The disciples were excited and full of emotion as they realized Jesus was alive, and they wanted to tell everyone.

Birth—Shepherds (a smelly job) were generally thought by the culture to be thieves and liars, considered to be untrustworthy and disrespected. (However, we have no way of knowing these particular shepherds were like the stereotype.) Social outcasts were the first to see and hear.

Resurrection—Many of Jesus' disciples had been common fishermen (a smelly job) and one was even a hated tax collector. A prostitute who had met Jesus and changed her lifestyle became one of His closest friends. Social outcasts were the first to see and hear.

Birth—The stable in Bethlehem was an important element of the Christmas story. Many theologians believe the manger where Joseph took his new family was actually a cave where animals were kept for shelter.

Resurrection—The tomb, likely a hewn-out cave in rock, was an important element of the resurrection story. Joseph of Arimathea and others prepared Jesus' body as that of any deceased person, then placed Him inside the tomb and rolled a large stone in front to protect and seal the grave.

Birth—The stable/manger was borrowed from an innkeeper.

Resurrection—The tomb was also borrowed (for three days) from Joseph of Arimathea.

Birth—God used the census issued by Caesar Augustus to give historical proof of when and where Jesus was born.

Resurrection—Joseph of Arimathea's decision to ask for Jesus' body from the government and then to put Him in his own tomb helped to verify the location and proof of the burial and resurrection.

SAY:

One can wonder that if Joseph of Arimathea did truly believe Jesus' own words that He would rise again in three days, then he would have also believed he was only loaning his tomb to Jesus!

There may have been no room in this fallen world for a Savior to be born, but the tomb was made empty so our hearts could be full!

DISCUSS:

- Why do you suppose God would be sure there were so many prophesies for all of Jesus' life, including His birth and death?

- Discuss the similarities between the angel's involvement in Christ's birth and resurrection, found in Luke 2:8–9, 13–14 and Matthew 28:1–5.

- Discuss the similarities of the cloth found in Luke 2:7 and John 20:3–7.

- Take a few minutes to discuss each of the A-B points about Christ's birth and resurrection.

- Why do you think God would go to so much trouble to match up such great detail between these two events about His Son?

SAY:

Reviewing this fascinating information about Christ's birth and resurrection, we must consider all the people who encountered Jesus throughout His three-year ministry. People seemed to either love Him deeply or hate Him with a passion. Peter was ready to die for Him in the garden when the soldiers came, yet Judas sold Him out and handed Him over to be crucified that same night—and both had been among His closest friends.

Why did Jesus create such controversy? Such division? Because He came to show the ultimate difference between the kingdom of God and the kingdom of Satan, to display the ultimate difference between light and darkness.

READ:

"Whoever acknowledges me before others, I will also acknowledge before my Father in heaven. But whoever disowns me before others, I will disown before my Father in heaven. Do not suppose that I have come to bring peace to the earth. I did not come to bring peace, but a sword." (Matthew 10:32–34)

SAY:

Jesus did not mean a literal sword, but that He would forever create the largest *dividing* line among humanity—those who believe in Him and those who don't. At the same time, He offers the greatest *unifying* factor ever experienced in the universe—His love and grace. If Christ Himself causes such reactions, you also will sometimes see similar responses to your faith should you follow Him. If you choose to live in His ways, people will question, reject, and criticize you too. This is inevitable. On the contrary, however, some people will be drawn to Christ in you, giving you the opportunity to share who He is and what He has done in your life.

READ:

Mary Magdalene went to the disciples with the news: "I have seen the Lord!" And she told them that he had said these things to her. (John 20:18)

A week later his disciples were in the house again, and Thomas was with them. Though the doors were locked, Jesus came and stood among them and said, "Peace be with you!" Then he said to Thomas, "Put your finger here; see my hands. Reach out your hand and put it into my side. Stop doubting and believe." Thomas said to him, "My Lord and my God!" (John 20:26–28)

SAY:

Mary's sorrow and grief turned to excitement and relief after she saw the risen Jesus. The disciples' fear and confusion changed to joy and peace after Jesus entered the room. Thomas' doubt and disbelief turned to faith and fact when he put his fingers on Jesus' wounds. We can experience the full life in Christ when we make Thomas' confession: "My Lord and my God!" John 20:31 sums up why God sent Jesus for *three years* of ministry and why He went through all He did in those *three days* before the resurrection.

READ:

"Jesus performed many other signs in the presence of his disciples, which are not recorded in this book. But these are written that you may believe that Jesus is the Messiah, the Son of God, and that by believing you may have life in his name."

SAY:

God has provided so much evidence and continuity in the story of Jesus. All these details are intended to deepen our faith and create awe that God would make Himself so clearly available. But these are all just interesting facts and trivia if they don't do a work in our hearts and deepen our love and commitment to Him. All the historical records, prophesies, and historians' and theologians' writings are not what change our lives. Those are simply *information for the mind*. What changes us is *transformation of the heart*.

WRAP-UP:

When you have completed the session, hit play on the video link, taking the video off pause, to watch the closing segment. If you cannot access the video, the basic script is available below to close the session.

As Jesus' ministry was impacting more and more people, there was debate and confusion as to who He actually was. There is an important account recorded in the gospels where Jesus asks His own disciples, "Who are people saying I am?" As they begin answering Him, He gets very personal. "Who do *you* say I am?" Awkward pause. Then Peter speaks up and says, "You are the Messiah sent from God." In short, Peter was saying, "I'm convinced You are who You say You are." (Matthew 16, Mark 8, Luke 9)

Jesus tells Peter a curious thing. He says, "Man didn't reveal this to you but God did. Because of this, I'll be able to build my church from your life."

If Jesus is God, if He was and is "the way, the truth, and the life," then every person must decide what to do about Him. So now it's your turn. Jesus asks you, "Who do your family and friends say I am?" As you begin to answer, He looks deep into your eyes and asks, "Okay, but what about you? Who do you say I am?"

WHAT IF THERE IS A PLAN FOR MY LIFE?

INTRODUCTION:

Begin by accessing and watching the opening video. Below we have provided both a QR code (accessible by a phone or tablet via a QR reader app) and a web link to type into an Internet browser. Should you not have access to the web, the basic script is also below.

After you watch the first section of the video, instructions will appear on the screen that says "Pause Program Now." Pause the video, allowing the logo to stay on the screen during the session. When you have completed the session, click play on the video to watch the closing segment.

http://ishinelive.com/shockandawepart4/

Welcome to iShine's *Shock & Awe's* fourth and final session. This last time together is going to be powerful as we bring all the questions—and answers—back around to zoom in on your life.

Why am *I* here?

Is there a big picture?

Is there more to life than *this*?

Is there a purpose for *me*?

What if *I* am a part of *God's* plan?

These are questions everyone asks—often. While we may never voice them out loud, we scream them in our soul. There might never be a time in history where more people are asking these very questions in our all-about-me, self-focused, selfie-crazed culture.

The truly amazing thing—and good news—is that these questions have already been answered. Sure, maybe not in the way most of us would think or even like, but they *are* answered. And these solutions are completely connected to the first three questions we covered:

- Is there a God?
- Is the Bible true?
- Is Christ who He claimed to be?

So let's get started. *The Shock & Awe* fourth and final question is: What if there is a plan for my life?

STUDY START

READ:

In the Disney movie *Tuck Everlasting,* a family discovers the fountain of youth. They become eternal beings, forever locked into the age at which they first drank the spring's water. A young lady named Winnie, who has befriended the family, discovers their secret and wants to drink from the water too. The Tuck father tells her, "If there's one thing I've learned about people, it's that they will do anything—anything—not to die. And they'll do anything to keep from living their life. What we Tucks have, you can't call it living. We just are. We're like rocks, stuck at the side of a stream. Don't be afraid of death, Winnie. Be afraid of the unlived life." [13]

🔑 SAY:

The problem we have with life that causes us to ask all these deep questions is not that it has a beginning, but because it has an end! Think about it: If you were alive forever on this earth, living as an immortal, why would you be concerned about your purpose? The fact that we know at any time something could happen and this life is over makes us look for meaning in our days. So, fully aware we don't have forever in this life, we ask: "Why am I here? What's the plan for me?"

When you get close to graduating from high school, what will everyone start asking you? ... "What's next?"

When you get close to graduating college, what will everyone ask you? ... "What's next?"

As a young single adult, what will everyone ask you? ... "When do you think you'll get married?"

After you're married, what will everyone ask you? ... "When will you have kids?"

Fast-forward to the season after someone retires. Even then we ask, "What's next?"

On and on through life, the question comes, on constant repeat. Until we die, we ask each other, "What's next?" But then there's the burning question everyone has of "What's next?" after we die!

From age eighteen to eighty, what we are really asking each other with the question of "What's next?" is:

- "What are you doing with your life?"
- "What's the point of your existence?"
- "How are you going to matter?"

The end is what makes life so valuable and crucial. We don't know how much time we have. Every day, any day, could be the last. We just don't know. This creates an urgency that few embrace; in fact, most ignore it. So many live denying the end is coming.

When you're young, it's really easy to live like you have sixty or seventy years ahead of you, and statistics prove that *may* be true. But still, no one knows. We all assume we're the exception. But this is also why when a young person is tragically killed, it is so devastating to family, friends, and the community. It drives home the reality of a short-lived life.

But as Mr. Tuck told Winnie, what is most tragic is the "unlived life." We want to live, not un-live! Linda Ellis wrote a poem simply called "The Dash." She refers to the birth year and the death year engraved on every headstone, but writes the line: "What mattered most of all was the dash between those years." When she writes and speaks, she encourages people with this advice: "Live your dash!"[14]

DISCUSS:

- Why do we tend to be more afraid of death than "the unlived life"?

- Why do you think we are always curious as to "what's next" for people?

- Why do you suppose so many people live from life event to life event?

- Why might a long "unlived life" be worse than a short-lived full life?

READ:

In 1642, Anthony van Diemen, Governor-General of the Dutch East Indies, commissioned Abel Tasman, a sea captain for the Dutch East India Company, to launch out on a voyage in search of unknown lands. The goal was to create maps of the unexplored regions south of the known world.

On this long journey, Tasman discovered what is now Tasmania and New Zealand. While these two landmasses were certainly worthwhile to find, on his first expedition Tasman somehow missed what would have been his biggest discovery—the largest island in the world, Australia. [15]

While there is a small national park named after Tasman in New Zealand, and in 1856 the nation he discovered was formally named "Tasmania" after him, what greater things might he be recognized for had he been the first to find Australia? Who knows? Australia might have been named Tasmania! [16]

SAY:

There is great irony in a legendary explorer being known just as much for what he *missed* as for what he *found*. When we hear the tale of Tasman, it is easy to question, "How in the world could he miss a landmass the size of Australia?"

Well, millions of people live life like Tasman explored—always searching, finding just enough to "get on the map" but actually missing the bigger picture.

We find this ongoing frustration regarding life, the chasing of satisfaction and contentment, and the quest for purpose in all of history's literature, music, and the arts. Even the Bible has expressions of this struggle. Listen to the words of Solomon, widely known as being the wisest man on earth due to God's blessing.

READ:

"Meaningless! Meaningless!" says the Teacher. "Utterly meaningless! Everything is meaningless." What do people gain from all their labors at which they toil under the sun? Generations come and generations go, but the earth remains forever. ... All things are wearisome, more than one can say. The eye never has enough of seeing, nor the ear its fill of hearing. What has been will be again, what has been done will be done again; there is nothing new under the sun. Is there anything of which one can say, "Look! This is something new"? It was here already, long ago; it was here before our time. No one remembers the former generations, and even those yet to come will not be remembered by those who follow them. (Ecclesiastes 1:2–4, 8–11)

SAY:

While it is so easy to complain about the "meaninglessness" of life, here's some good news: The answer to the question "Why am I here?" has already been answered for each of us.

But this answer comes to us as a private choice, not a public command. God wants to help you discover all He created you to be. He wants to involve you in His life and work. Today. Right now. He wants you to make a difference in thousands of other lives. He wants to empower you to move His kingdom forward and defeat the work of the enemy. That's exactly what redemption means, taking something headed the wrong way, led by self, and turning it around for good, led by God. But it's not a demand He makes but a choice He offers.

READ:

So you should look for the Lord before it is too late; you should call to him while he is near. The wicked should stop doing wrong, and they should stop their evil thoughts. They should return to the Lord so he may have mercy on them. They should come to our God, because he will freely forgive them. (Isaiah 55:6–7 NCV)

SAY:

But what happens when we say yes to the choice, to His offer, and do exactly what Isaiah says to do?

Look at Jesus' disciples. We see an amazing transformation in their lives from the day they dropped their nets to the days after Jesus ascended into heaven as they began preaching and healing in His name. We see normal men and women daily living out a supernatural lifestyle. What happened to them? The life of Jesus became their life. His ways became their ways. His truth became their truth; the exact same thing God wants to do with you.

If faith in Christ is going to be real—not American-cultural-religious but real like the disciples'—it can't be just an item on your weekly to-do list. It's not *on* your checklist—it *is* the list!

Think about a waffle. Golden brown with a grid of perfect little compartments. That is often how we think of our lives. We have our family compartment, friend compartment, school compartment, social media compartment, fun compartment, and church compartment. And often we think they all have nice, convenient walls so none of them actually touch or connect to the others.

Family has no connection to friends. Social media has nothing to do with school. Fun has nothing to do with church.

But here comes the syrup, pouring out onto and flowing over it all. Running down into and filling up every compartment, every single square, so now you don't see all those divided sections as much as you see a covered and saturated delicacy. That's a very simple analogy of Jesus covering our lives. He doesn't go neatly into one or two little squares and stay there; that is religion. He soaks, drenches, and floods our entire being, connecting all of life through a relationship with Him; that's authentic faith.

READ:

Love the Lord your God with all your heart and with all your soul and with all your strength. (Deuteronomy 6:5)

SAY:

We often think our body, soul, and mind are each in separate compartments, but loving God in every part of our being changes our entire life.

Listen to *The Message* version of this same verse.

READ:

Love God, your God, with your whole heart: love him with all that's in you, love him with all you've got! (Deuteronomy 6:5 MSG)

SAY:

Love God with all that is in you, with all you've got!

⚿ DISCUSS:

- How do you think the explorer Tasman's life is much like the lives of many people today who are searching for life's answers?

- Discuss the waffle analogy. Why do we see life in compartments much like waffle squares?

- Why would the mind, body, and spirit connection be crucial to loving God?

SAY:

Check out Matthew 6:33, expressed four different ways:

READ:

But seek first his kingdom and his righteousness, and all these things will be given to you as well.

But more than anything else, put God's work first and do what he wants. Then the other things will be yours as well. (CEV)

Seek the Kingdom of God above all else, and live righteously, and he will give you everything you need. (NLT)

Instead, be concerned above everything else with the Kingdom of God and with what he requires of you, and he will provide you with all these other things. (GNT)

⚷━━━ᴇ SAY:

This is a powerful verse because it contains an amazing promise from God.

If you're a Christian, you believe that when you die, you will have an eternal home in heaven, right? But God hasn't taken you there yet, so this has to mean that you must have some kind of purpose here, right now, something He wants you to do or accomplish *before* He takes you home. You have your "ticket" to heaven, but you're on a journey with Him now that has starts, stops, and adventures along the way.

In Matthew 6, Jesus was teaching a large crowd, telling them what His kingdom is all about. Let's take this verse apart to see what He's saying.

SEEK—The first word is *seek*. At the beginning of each Bible version, we see an action verb.

- See
- Put
- Be concerned

These words are directed at us, challenging us to:

- Go after
- Pursue
- Look for
- Prioritize

Have you ever played the game Hide & Seek? What does the seeker do? If you're seeking something, do you sit around and wait for it to come to you? No, you go after it. You take action. You're actively searching to find what you seek.

FIRST—Connected to these action verbs are the phrases:

- First
- More than anything else
- Above all else
- Above everything else

Do these phrases sound like you should "seek, put, or be concerned with" sometime later on when you have some free time? When you feel like it? When you want to? When everything else is done and you're bored? No, this is the language of priority. First is first. The first thing I do in all things is seek.

But seek *what* first?

KINGDOM—So what do you seek or place first? Your kingdom? Your parents' kingdom? Boyfriend or girlfriend's kingdom? Your church's kingdom? No. Whose kingdom? God's.

Unlike an earthly king's physical realm, God's kingdom is only visible in the lives of His followers who are doing the very thing we are talking about: seeking Him first. Placing their relationship with Him before anything else. Doing what He wants them to do. Obeying Him. God's kingdom is His people and His activity that surrounds their lives. Earthly kings have borders and boundaries; God does not.

RIGHTEOUSNESS—Next, we have the phrases:

- And his righteousness
- What He wants
- Live righteously
- What He requires of you

So what is righteousness? It is God's way to right, just, and holy living through His Son, Jesus Christ. It is God's way to live. What He wants. What He requires of you.

Whose righteousness is it? Yours? Ours? Your church's? Your pastor's? No. God's. Only His. We have no righteousness of our own.

READ:

For we have already shown that all people, whether Jews or Gentiles, are under the power of sin. As the Scriptures say, "No one is righteous—not even one. No one is truly wise; no one is seeking God. All have turned away; all have become useless. No one does good, not a single one." (Romans 3:9–12 NLT)

But God has made a way for you and me to be right with Him, for us to have a right relationship with a holy God. His name is Jesus—the only Source of righteousness. Moving down just a little further in Romans 3, we read:

But now God has shown us a way to be made right with him without keeping the requirements of the law, as was promised in the writings of Moses and the prophets long ago. We are made right with God by placing our faith in Jesus Christ. And this is true for everyone who believes, no matter who we are. (Romans 3:21–22 NLT)

SAY:

GOD GIVES—And, finally, the last part:
- And all these things will be given to you as well.
- Then the other things will be yours as well.
- He will give you everything you need.
- He will provide you with all these other things.

In our commercially driven, me-centered, materialistic world, we can often see God's giving nature or His gifts as His being some kind of cosmic Santa Claus. He can become just a formula to get what we want. In many circles of American Christian culture, God is a way to gain success or the relationship we want. We come to believe He can be manipulated toward our will.

This mindset is, of course, the furthest thing from the life of an authentic Christian disciple. In three of the four gospels, Jesus' sobering reminder to His followers is recorded as to what life with Him would cost. Here is one:

READ:

Then Jesus said to his disciples, "Whoever wants to be my disciple must deny themselves and take up their cross and follow me. For whoever wants to save their life will lose it, but whoever loses their life for me will find it." (Matthew 16:24–25)

Therefore, the challenge is for us to remain faithful to Him, yet when we fail—and we will—we seek forgiveness and move right back into relationship with Him, taking up our cross again to receive His life.

Let's review what we've seen in Matthew 6:33 so far: As a follower of Christ, you are to go after, to pursue, the very first thing before anything else—the kingdom of God. That's a very clear mission statement for a purpose in life.

DISCUSS:

- While we have so many good and important relationships in life, why would God tell us to seek Him first?

- How might we best find and fit into God's kingdom while here on earth?

- How does God's righteousness fit into this idea of us finding purpose in life?

- Discuss God's promise of adding or giving us all we need if we seek Him.

SAY:

For this verse to be fully understood, we must go back and see what Jesus is referring to when he says "all things." Leading up to verse 33, Matthew 6 contains the infamous "do not worry" passage. Here it is, verses 25–32:

READ:

I tell you not to worry about your life. Don't worry about having something to eat, drink, or wear. Isn't life more than food or clothing? Look at the birds in the sky! They don't plant or harvest. They don't even store grain in barns. Yet your Father in heaven takes care of them. Aren't you worth more than birds? Can worry make you live longer? Why worry about clothes? Look how the wild flowers grow. They don't work hard to make their clothes. But I tell you that Solomon with all his wealth wasn't as well clothed as one of them. God gives such beauty to everything that grows in the fields, even though it is here today and thrown into a fire tomorrow. He will surely do even more for you! Why do you have such little faith? Don't worry and ask yourselves, "Will we have anything to eat? Will we have anything to drink? Will we have any clothes to wear?" Only people who don't know God are always worrying about such things. Your Father in heaven knows that you need all of these. (CEV)

SAY:

When you seek God's kingdom first and His righteousness, then you won't have to worry about your life. God will take care of you—in every detail. Your purpose, the reason you are here, will be made clear to you.

Think on this question for a moment: Do you know anyone who lets God totally take care of him/her and doesn't seem to worry about the stuff everyone else does? Do you know anyone who is so God-focused that, while his/her life certainly isn't *perfect*, it always seems to be *peaceful?*

So many people today live with an entitlement attitude toward life, meaning they think everyone owes them something. So many also struggle with laziness and apathy, always taking the low road or the easy way in life.

The best path is to live like anything that anyone does for you is a blessing. Be grateful for all God gives, and you will find Him *and* His righteousness in that attitude.

The bottom line of Matthew 6:33 is: God is promising you that if you will take care of His mission here on earth, He will take care of you here and for eternity. You take care of His kingdom, and He'll take care of yours.

But then the "What's next?" question comes back to this question: How can we be sure we are taking care of God's mission?

READ:

In John 15:5–8, Jesus says, "Yes, I am the vine; you are the branches. Those who remain in me, and I in them, will produce much fruit. For apart from me you can do nothing. Anyone who does not remain in me is thrown away like a useless branch and withers. Such branches are gathered into a pile to be burned. But if you remain in me and my words remain in you, you may ask for anything you want, and it will be granted! When you produce much fruit, you are my true disciples. This brings great glory to my Father." (NLT)

In the Greek language, the word we translate as remain or *abide* is a key imperative in this passage, indicating that we are connected to Christ—the vine—by faith. In this relationship, He then will remain in us by His very nature, just as the vine holds the branches with no effort from the branches.

Notice that Jesus tells us to remain in Him, assuring us that He is faithful to keeping us clean, forgiven, and ready to bear fruit. He is committed to us, so we must stay committed to Him by faith.

Also, the last sentence in the first verse is crucial: "For apart from me, you can do nothing." This little phrase is critical in helping us understand how God works. So many people ask Christ into their lives, then go off on their own and start trying to do "good things" to impress Him and gain His approval.

But, as a Christian, you're not only found—you are also in His hand—forever! He will never leave you or forsake you. You can still leave Him, forsake and renounce Him, but He's all about you now. You already have His approval! You are so in!

This truth is the real meaning of life. True devotion to Christ will make life count like none other!

In an interview where Bono, the iconic lead singer of the rock band U2, was being asked about his faith and his many humanitarian works all around the world, he responded by saying, "A wise man once told me, 'Stop asking God to bless what you're doing. Get involved in what God is doing, because it's already blessed.'"[17]

So is there a master plan and you're in it? Yes! You're here to live for Christ, because He died for you. He loves you and now lives in you, so you and He make an amazing team that can, quite literally, change the world.

We must fully focus on our own "unlived life." God wants to give each of us a well-lived life. We can each have our own story of an amazing Lord who can do something we could never do without Him or on our own.

WRAP-UP:

When you have completed the session, hit play on the video link, taking the video off pause, to watch the closing segment. If you cannot access the video, the basic script is available below to close the session.

In John 8:28–29, Jesus gave us yet another glimpse into the vast depth of His love and commitment to the Father.

So Jesus said, "When you have lifted up the Son of Man on the cross, then you will understand that I am he. I do nothing on my own but say only what the Father taught me. And the one who sent me is with me—he has not deserted me. For I always do what pleases him." (NLT)

Wouldn't it be amazing to declare, "I only say what God tells me to say, and I only do what pleases the Father." The great news is we can! When we make the decision to follow Christ, then the One who made that declaration is living inside of us.

The closing questions for each of us to consider are ...

What *am* I focused on?

What *should* I be focused on?

What is going to change in my life if nothing changes?

What could change in my life if I give Jesus everything—all of me?

You can be a part of God's plan, so ... are you in?

BEGINNING A RELATIONSHIP WITH GOD THROUGH JESUS CHRIST

You may have the question, "So how do I begin a relationship with God?" First, and most important, we recommend you talk to a parent, pastor, or priest regarding this significant spiritual decision.

Since Adam and Eve's choice in the garden, all mankind has been born with a sin nature. The Bible defines sin as attitudes, thoughts, and actions that separate us from God. Even when we try to be "good," we still make selfish decisions outside of His will.

In Paul's letter to the Roman church, he lays out a clear path from our sin to Christ's salvation. Millions have found new life in these simple, profound truths.

For ever since the world was created, people have seen the earth and sky. Through everything God made, they can clearly see his invisible qualities—his eternal power and divine nature. So they have no excuse for not knowing God. Yes, they knew God, but they wouldn't worship him as God or even give him thanks. And they began to think up foolish ideas of what God was like. As a result, their minds became dark and confused. (Romans 1:20–21)

We are made right with God by placing our faith in Jesus Christ. And this is true for everyone who believes, no matter who we are. For everyone has sinned; we all fall short of God's glorious standard. (Romans 3:22–23)

But God showed his great love for us by sending Christ to die for us while we were still sinners. (Romans 5:8)

For the wages of sin is death, but the free gift of God is eternal life through Christ Jesus our Lord. (Romans 6:23)

If you openly declare that Jesus is Lord and believe in your heart that God raised him from the dead, you will be saved. For it is by believing in your heart that you are made right with God, and it is by openly declaring your faith that you are saved. (Romans 10:9–10)

For, "Everyone who calls on the name of the Lord will be saved." (Romans 10:13)

While these verses offer the simple truth of the Gospel, God gives you the freedom to choose. If you are ready to make your choice, a parent, priest, or pastor would love to talk with you about this important decision and answer any questions.

We would also love to hear from you at info@bemamedia.com.

For I am not ashamed of this Good News about Christ. It is the power of God at work, saving everyone who believes—the Jew first and also the Gentile. (Romans 1:16)

ENDNOTES

1 J. P. Moreland, Creation Hypothesis (Downer's Grove, IL: InterVarsity Press, 1994), 273.

2 Kyle Butt, "Design Demands a Designer," 2002, Apologetics Press: http://apologeticspress.org/apcontent.aspx?category=9&article=877.

3 Live Science Staff, "Purpose of Fingerprints is Questioned," June 17, 2009, Live Science: http://www.livescience.com/3684-purpose-fingerprints-questioned.html.

4 Scott M. Huse, The Collapse of Evolution (Grand Rapids, MI: Baker Books, 2008), 87–88.

5 Gillian Hammerton, "The Ceiling of the Sistine Chapel, The Vatican, Rome, Michelangelo," June 20, 2012, Michelangelo: http://michelangelllogreat.blogspot.com.

6 "How We Got the Bible," Bible.org: https://bible.org/book/export/html/6419.

7 "Why Bible Translation?" 2015, Wycliffe: https://www.wycliffe.org/about/why.

8 Wayne Jackson, "How Many Prophecies Are in the Bible?" Christian Courier: https://www.christiancourier.com/articles/318-how-many-prophecies-are-in-the-bible.

9 "1456 Gutenberg Produces the First Printed Bible," 1990, Christianity Today: http://www.christianitytoday.com/history/issues/issue-28/1456-gutenberg-produces-first-printed-bible.html.

10 Daniel Burke, "How Many Versions of the Bible Do We Really Need?" Christianity.com: http://www.christianity.com/bible/how-many-versions-of-the-bible-do-we-really-need-11639814.html.

11 J. Warner Wallace, "Is There Any Evidence for Jesus Outside the Bible?" May 1, 2014, Cold-Case Christianity: http://coldcasechristianity.com/2014/is-there-any-evidence-for-jesus-outside-the-bible/.

12 Ibid.

13 "Tuck Everlasting Quotes," 2002, IMDb: http://www.imdb.com/title/tt0283084/quotes.

14 Linda Ellis, "The Dash," 1996, linda-ellis.com: http://www.linda-ellis.com/the-dash-the-dash-poem-by-linda-ellis-.html.

15 "Abel Tasman," February 3, 2016, New World Encyclopedia: http://www.newworldencyclopedia.org/p/index.php?title=Abel_Tasman&oldid=993780.

16 "Tasmania History," About Australia: http://www.about-australia.com/tasmania-history/.

17 Bono, "Transcript: Bono Remarks at the National Prayer Breakfast," February 2, 2006, USA Today: http://usatoday30.usatoday.com/news/washington/2006-02-02-bono-transcript_x.htm.